YOU KNOW YOU ARE

A LUTHERAN IF...

By Janet Letnes Martin and Suzann (Johnson) Nelson

Printed in the United States of America

*Published by Caragana Press
Box 396
Hastings, Minnesota 55033*

ISBN 1-1886627-09-6
Second Edition Third Printing 2006
Cover Design: Joe Gillaspie   *Printer: Sentinel Printing*
Hastings, MN   *St. Cloud, MN*

DEDICATION

This little book is dedicated to Martin Luther's gang who stayed faithful to the Lutheran heritage even though members hopped around some among synods, merged some, dropped some, and created new ones.

Dedicated to the members — past and present — of the: NLCA, LCN, LCD, ALC, ELC, LFC, LCA, AALC, CLBA, CLC, LCC, EFCA, TALC, LCMS, AFLC, ULCA, ELS, WELS, ELCIC, CoLC, TAALC, ELCM, ALCA, DELC, ELCC, LMS-USA, CLA, ELCA, and to the ultramodern Lutherans who think it's okay to mix and merge with the Episcopalians, even though it will just turn us into a bunch of "Lute-piskers."

This is most certainly true!

TABLE OF CONTENTS

TO OUR FELLOW LUTHERANS...

We hope you have as much fun reading this book as we had writing it. (It was much easier than taking Sermon Notes.) We could have written many more pages with all the material we dug out of our Lutheran Brains, but we will just have to write a sequel.

While writing this book we came to the realization that Lutherans are right there swimming along in the politically correct mainstream in that <u>we are diverse!</u> This is most certainly true!

Now this may surprise many of you. You think we all have blue eyes, blonde hair and thick arms. Well, most of us have blue eyes, blonde hair and thick arms, but our diversity shows not in our appearance, but rather in our faith. There are as many kinds of Lutherans as there are valleys in Norway. We really are a "particular people" as the theme for the 1967 National Lutheran League Convention proclaimed. (This is the convention where dancing was demoted from the category of sin.)

In this book you'll find your preferred brand of Lutheranism . . . from those who never bothered to find out where the money in the Birthday Bank really went, to those who think it is perfectly normal to serve salsa in a Lutheran Church basement.

While most Lutherans continue to split and merge, we try to figure out important details of our heritage such as: Did Martin Luther really do the chicken dance at his wedding? Hopefully this book will help you lighten up, laugh (even if you're a German Lutheran and believe a sense of humor is one of the seven deadly sins), and celebrate your heritage.

Janet and Suzann

YOU KNOW YOU ARE A STEADFAST
LUTHERAN IF . . .

YOU KNOW YOU ARE A STEADFAST LUTHERAN IF...

You don't think Martin Luther actually wanted to start a new religion, but he just got all fed up and couldn't take it any more so he started scribbling and pounding like a stubborn German would, and he got carried away and one thing led to another and you recognize the feeling and pretty soon he was standing out in front of the church pounding up his 95 theses and shouting, "Here I stand!", with a black and blue fingernail to boot, and life has never been the same.

You wonder why Martin, as long as he

had taken the time to write 95 theses, didn't round it off to an even 100?

You know that Luther's Rose belongs on a lapel, not in a vase.

You know better than to question the pastor or synod hotshots openly even though Martin Luther sure would have if he were still alive.

You know perfectly well why there is no Lutheran Church named Good Works Lutheran.

You think the phrase "Lutheran Bishop" is an oxymoron.

You wholeheartedly believe the cardinal rule: Lutherans don't sit in the front two pews.

You consider a "different" church one where the organ is on the right side and the piano is on the left.

You remember the first and middle initials of all the pastors back to the day your congregation was founded.

You still refer to the pastor who has faithfully served your congregation for twelve years as "the new minister."

Your pastor is about as flexible as a monument in the cemetery.

You feel that pastors got more respect when they wore black robes and got two dead, dressed-out chickens and a ham from the congregation at Christmas rather than a pension.

You really have a tough time with the idea that pastors and missionaries procreate.

You get suspicious when the pastor doesn't give one of his kids a Biblical first name.

You believe that any pastor's wife worth her salt can play the piano and/or fluteo-phone and will gladly do so for Sunday School and Ladies Aid and for any number of budding, or over-the-hill, soloists.

You feel that Sunday School started going to pot when the assembled body quit singing **The Lord is In His Holy Temple** as a mandatory convening song.

You know what a flannelgraph board is.

You can name the ancestors, back to the third and fourth generation, of the Christmas and Easter two-timer crowd that shows up and takes your pew.

You keep your family genealogy in the Old Family Bible just like everyone else so that no one will find it and figure out that your great-grandparents "had to get married".

You can sing at least the first verse of two Christmas hymns in a foreign language— German, Norwegian or Swedish.

You are in your eighties and can still recite at least three of your Sunday School Christmas pieces and know what grades you were in when you were a shepherd and a wiseman, and what grade you were in when you were roped into playing Joseph, and you still remember who was Mary that year, and secretly wonder if she still looks good in blue.

You wonder who plays Mary in the Christmas Program in congregations where the pastor doesn't have any daughters.

You keep your Baptismal Certificate with your Lutheran Brotherhood (LB) or AAL insurance policy in a safe, dry place.

Your Baptismal Certificate is a whole booklet filled with Bible verses and angelic pictures and is signed by the church secretary who used the Palmer

Penmanship Method – not a one-pager form filled in on a computer.

You not only know who your Baptismal Sponsors were but you also remember them with a little something at Christmas.

You find your Cradle Roll Certificate packed neatly among well-preserved crepe paper nutcups left over from Mother-Daughter Banquets when you clean out your parents' house.

You wax nostalgic when you see little red or brown wooden chairs.

You crave beverages that come from a Watkins bottle.

You know that the phrase "Opening Exercises" didn't refer to something physical.

You hear that the Sunday School is thinking about purchasing a DVD player and you immediately start thinking about men's underwear.

You hear news coverage about the Rainbow Coalition and immediately start humming **Jesus Loves the Little Children.**

You had to read <u>Gopher Tails for Papa</u> in Sunday School.

As a form of religious art, you prefer Oletta Wold's silhouettes over

Michelangelo's paintings.

You never questioned where the money in the Birthday Bank went, and subconsciously you still save your pennies for it.

You can recite the names of the Books of the Bible just as easily as you can say "Now is the time for all good men to come to the aid of their party".

You believe Vacation Bible School and Watkins Nectar go together like love and marriage or a horse and carriage. In other words, you can't have one without the other!

You think that playing cards at Bible Camp is pushing the sanctioned activity list a little too far.

You are pretty sure that a Sock Hop is just a disguised dance without shoes on.

You believe that dancing should not be a part of a Lutheran wedding celebration because the **Bunny Hop** and **Macarena** aren't in any of the many hymnals.

You are almost positive that when Salome danced before the king it must have been the **Chicken Dance**.

You are still trying to reconcile Thou Shalt Not Drink with having wine for communion.

You're sure the wine at the Wedding of Cana was Welch's Grape Juice.

You still call Confirmation classes "reading for the minister".

You have uttered the phrases, "What Does This Mean?", "How Is This Done?" and "This Is Most Certainly True" more times than you care to remember.

You learned what words like beseech,

besmirch, backbite, stricken, smitten and afflicted mean and they still produce guilt in you.

You think it is unnecessary for teens to travel 500 miles from home to learn how to become a better Christian.

You would rather have your offspring become a member of the Concert Choir at Augsburg, St. Olaf, Concordia, Wartburg, Waldorf, Luther, Dana or Augustana than be either a millionaire or the President of the United States.

You still have the corsage from your church basement bridal shower, a Chore Boy backed by a fanned dishrag with measuring spoons inserted to make it both festive and practical.

You know who all the stained glass windows were given in memory of, what year the windows were installed, what the person died from, who sang at the funeral, what the weather was like the day of the funeral, and whether or not it was a large funeral.

You know that "glads" are funeral flowers.

You feel you have done your part for the grieving family when you say something deeply profound at funerals like, "Oh, he looks so natural," or "I think she was about my age," or "They did such a nice job on him," or "Sure thought she'd make it through Christmas".

You judge the purity of a congregation by the color of its hymnal.

You think "The Baptism Song" is a synonym for **Children of the Heavenly Father.**

You don't sing **Shout for Joy, Loud and Long** (<u>WOV</u> #793) very well but you can sure squeak out – and feel – **O Sacred Head Now Wounded** (<u>Black</u> #315).

You don't sing anything from <u>WOV</u> very

well.

You refer to every county not by name but simply as "overseas".

You understand the meaning of **Bringing in the Sheaves** even though you had a baler.

You see nothing wrong with serving

finger sandwiches after a missionary slide show about Christianity's Effect on Cannibalism.

You still blush when you open a copy of <u>National Geographic</u>, figure it must be some form of porno-lite, and are thankful it is mailed out in a plain brown wrapper.

You can sing **Fishers of Men** in Swahili and still remember all the arm movements to **Away in a Manger**.

Your grandchildren can find Tanganyika, Zululand, North Borneo, Madagascar and Norway on the map blindfolded, but don't have a clue where Chicago, Las Vegas, France or Italy are located.

You often wonder why they are called mission "fields" when it is apparent from viewing filmstrips at Family Night that there are no fields or even crops.

You support all the missions you can but you don't think it is necessary to witness at the County Fair to the carnies because it won't do any good, especially to those whose earrings are bigger than their short shorts.

You never mistakenly think "Upper G-I" when you hear the word "tract".

You get a little nervous watching filmstrips of the mission fields for fear that the pedal pushers you gave to the clothing drive might just show up on the screen.

You've been faithfully working on mission quilts for 35 years but deep down wonder if it isn't too hot to use them in Africa.

You truly believe that wafers are more sacred than hunks of bread for Communion.

You secretly wonder just who goes

downtown to the local hard liquor store to buy the Communion wine.

You get somewhat twitchy at Communion when a female pastor wearing earrings is administering it.

You are certain that a Common Cup is for the field, not the sanctuary.

You wish the politically-correct gender police would have left The Creed, The Lord's Prayer, and good old standard hymns alone.

You wonder why they had to dumb down the liturgy by changing "the quick and the dead" to "the living and the dead".

You seriously feel that your body and

brain cannot take one more discussion about mergers, new hymnals or the ecumenical movement.

You can name at least six Lutheran Synods and which people left in a huff but can't tell the theological differences among them.

You are concerned that Lutherans won't

quit compiling and promoting hymnals until there is one to match each color in Joseph's coat.

You think that Lutherans merging with the Episcopalians would create just a bunch of "Lute-piskers" running around.

You still call it <u>The New Red Hymnal</u>.

You sometimes think everyday is A Day of Humiliation and Prayer as referred to in <u>The New Red Hymnal</u>.

You have never questioned the theology of the Marriage Ceremony in <u>The New Red Hymnal</u>.

Your pastor starts in on the "We beseech thee to hear us, good Lord" canned prayers that were introduced in <u>The New Red Hymnal</u> and you glance at your Confirmation Bulova and make bets in your mind if he is going to do four, six or all twelve.

You start to wonder about the Separation of Church and State when your pastor gets to the sixth "beseech thee prayer" in <u>The New Red Hymnal</u>.

You're a little bit curious why there are so many French carols and folksongs in the various Lutheran hymnbooks.

You secretly understand that antiphonal readings were introduced into the Lutheran Church to either hang on to young males whose voices were changing or to accommodate kids who lacked the discipline to learn to carry a tune.

You know what pages **Beautiful Savior** is on in <u>The Black</u>, <u>New Red</u>, <u>Green</u>, <u>Concordia</u> and <u>Youth Sings</u> books and don't care what page it is on in <u>With One Voice</u> (WOV).

You know that a soft-covered hymnal is really just a song book.

You still are uncomfortable reciting

some of the liturgical phrases like *gloria in excelsis, gloria patri* and *agnus dei* because they sound Catholic.

You still, under your breath, say "Holy Christian Church" when <u>The Green Hymnal</u> clearly states "holy catholic church."

You would rather tour Augsburg

Publishing House than the Library of Congress.

You remember where you were when you saw your first nun.

You secretly admire the bravery of Catholics who can admit their sins out loud to another person.

You are thankful that none of the Lutheran colleges are within easy biking distance of St. Cloud, MN.

You know what the term "To Turn" means and who lost their inheritance rights to the farm because they did.

You have strong beliefs and your own ideas but never question things out loud.

You're pretty sure you know which people in your congregation have fallen prey to one of the seven deadly sins.

You know that the only acceptable reasons for skipping Sunday Services are hospitalization and when your cows are out.

You know a thing or two about church

etiquette and know you don't sit down after standing during the service unless the pastor tells you to do so.

You are certain that all the pairs of animals in Noah's Ark are married.

You vote against purchasing a computer for the church office and then when it arrives you refer to it as a key-punch.

You can't figure out why they changed "trespasses" to "debts." "Trespasses" reminded you that you could have been hunting instead of sitting in church, and "debts" reminds you of your Visa card balance and then they have the gall to ask you to up your pledge.

You are perfectly aware that God is omnipresent and the Creator of Heaven and Earth, yet you automatically twinge a little bit when you receive an invitation to an outdoor wedding to be held at a golf course and kind of wonder, just for a split second, what Apostle Paul would think.

You get extremely fidgety when the words "pray out loud," "testimony" or "altar call" are mentioned.

Your favorite Beatitude is "Blessed are the Meek" and you know it is referring to those who are uncomfortable being asked to shake hands with the next person or that it has something to do with <u>The Green Hymnal</u> idea of "passing the peace".

You get uncomfortable meeting someone who has been described as "outgoing".

You feel that "passing the peace" is a little bit too touchy-feely and is better left to the Pentecostal groups.

You feel that altar calls are for show-offs, the weak or the weepy, and are better suited to another religion.

You've been tempted more than once to blurt out, "Well, I don't give a rip!" at Annual Meetings but know you never could.

You leave the Annual Meeting about as ruffled as the pastor's collar in the Old Country.

You often leave church more worked up

than when you arrived.

You know that dancing and playing pool are sins, but roller skating and playing shuffleboard are not, and you have never considered the similarities.

You don't see anything wrong with a little shame, and vote to publish in the back of the Annual Report what everyone gave to the church .

Your favorite phrases are "What is, is" and "Because we have always done it this way".

You get a little confused when the adult Bible study is going to be about euthanasia and you recall that when you were little most of the Sunday School

Birthday Bank money went to missionaries in China who were helping the youth in Asia.

You would rather have your son-in-law be a laid-off ,over-the-road trucker than a bigshot at Synod Headquarters.

You were hurt deeply and disillusioned when you learned that Billy Graham,

Lawrence Welk, the Lennon Sisters, Chet Huntley, Dale Warland and Arthur Godfrey weren't Lutheran.

You think that someone as decent and wholesome as Lawrence Welk could have made a fine living without showing champagne bubbles floating over the television screen.

You just understand that it goes without saying that Merrill Krantzen's barn burned down on Tuesday evening because Merrill was out plowing the Sunday before.

You head up a committee to install a lit cross on the steeple to secretly compete with the Christmas star the co-op board placed on top of the local grain elevator.

You know which grocery store, gas station and car dealer in town is the Norwegian-Lutheran one and which are the Swedish-Lutheran and you shop appropriately regardless of price.

You see various kinds of cars and tractors as Lutheran, Methodist or Catholic-owned.

You know that if you don't want to be called upon to give devotions at church you'll wear a V-necked dress.

You are uncomfortable with female ushers and men doing dishes in the church basement.

You know that God didn't create snakes or dust; Satan did.

You wonder why they didn't edit words like dancing, tambourine, ass and breast out of the Bible.

You kind of think of soft-covered Bibles as a condensed <u>Readers Digest</u> version. You read it through in '62, but probably should dust it off again in '02.

YOU KNOW YOU ARE A LUTHERAN CHURCH BASEMENT WOMAN IF...

YOU KNOW YOU ARE A LUTHERAN CHURCH BASEMENT WOMAN IF...

You realize that WELCA is just a fancy modern name for Ladies Aid, i.e., "a rose by any other name is still a rose".

You believe it would be easier to be a colonel in the Army than to be President of the Ladies Aid.

You realize that there is usually at least one Ladies Aid President who has let her power "go to her head".

You understand the caste system of who the Marys are and who the Marthas are and that you can't cross over unless you marry well.

You would like to yell "get some of the younger ones to do it," but rather you say, "you bet I can work, I have nothing better to do".

You know how "to do a doings".

You know exactly what it feels like when the Jell-O melts into the scalloped potatoes on a paper plate.

You know instinctively that grape Jell-O isn't going to cut it for church doings.

You know "red arms" has nothing to do with Communists but with mashing hundreds of pounds of potatoes for the

Lutefisk Supper.

You get so pooped out from boiling potatoes and fish for the *Lutefisk* Supper that you feel a close kinship to 90-year-old Sarah in the Bible when she was in labor.

You wonder if Ladies Aid meetings in heaven will be ecumenical, and if so, will the women from North Borneo wear proper foundation garments at the meetings or just let it all hang out as you have seen on missionary slides.

You get a little nervous when the Pastor's wife walks into the kitchen.

You get real nervous when the Pastor himself walks into the kitchen.

You are one of four women who looks up and straightens your apron when the Pastor calls out, "Bertha".

You know that church basements should be painted mint green and beige, and nurseries should be painted yellow.

You attend a church that has funeral tablecloths, hooks on the kitchen door for hanging purses, and a locked sugar-lump cupboard.

You realize there is no place in a church kitchen for chairs, but every Lutheran kitchen must have two stools for buttering buns.

You could walk into the church kitchen blindfolded and open the drawer where the LB or AAL napkins are kept.

You have been pinched by the leg braces when taking down the church basement tables.

You figure that if Pepsi and Kodak can be Official Olympic Sponsors then Watkins Nectar and Air Wick should be Official Lutheran Sponsors.

Your favorite white food is lard.

You know that nuts and mints are only served at wedding and anniversary celebrations and not for "everday" doings, and that a wedding without mints, mixed nuts and sandwich loaf could just as well have taken place before the Justice of the Peace.

You know the nectar supply has to be checked out before Vacation Bible School starts.

You believe that sugar lumps should be a separate line item in the Ladies Aid budget.

You don't think it is unusual for someone to be specifically assigned to butter buns and slice pickles at any doings.

You would suffer from guilt if you didn't evenly divide up the leftover bars, hotdish buns and pickles with all those who served at a funeral.

You don't think 14 hotdishes, 12 kinds Jell-O and six kinds of pickles spread out on the serving counter is overkill.

You don't need to look in a cookbook to make a funeral hotdish for fifty.

You volunteer to edit the Ladies Aid cookbook so you can insert "cut up chicken pieces" and delete "cut up chicken breasts," and remove the sherry that is called for in recipes submitted by Contemporary Lutheran women who live in town and don't own property.

You think tuna hotdish is okay, but fishsticks are a little too ecumenical.

You don't have to think twice about how many eggs, how much coffee or how much water are needed to make a five-gallon white enameled pot of coffee.

You have at least four recipes for watermelon rind pickles and three recipes for beet pickles.

You know by heart how many jars of pickles it takes to serve 154 mourners at a funeral.

You know the difference between funeral and Ladies Aid size cuts when serving church basement cakes and bars.

You know that funeral meat, commonly called "dead spreads," is always minced ham or Spam on white bread, egg salad on wheat bread, and Cheese Whiz and olives on rye bread.

You mark your bar pans and hotdish bowls with red fingernail polish and then forget to take them home from church.

You bring your Jell-O to the basement in the green Pyrex bowl covered with a "pantry panty".

You bring your hotdish to the basement in the yellow Pyrex bowl wrapped and tied up in a big white cotton dishtowel.

You always have a few loaves of banana bread and a few pan of bars in the freezer at home, just in case.

You know that anyone named Agnes brings really good bars to church.

You know that someone who coined the name "bars" couldn't have been a real Lutheran.

You know that anyone who calls hotdish

a covered dish or casserole wasn't born
and raised in a Lutheran community in
the Midwest.

You have resigned yourself to the fact
that the State Fair Lutheran Lunch Stand
is a necessary evil.

You think of beet pickles, *lefse* and tuna
hotdish when you hear a BLT ordered in

a restaurant.

You have a specific pair of shoes that you only use for serving funerals, weddings and *Lutefisk* Suppers.

You know how tuckered out Jesus must have been after feeding the 5,000 and secretly wonder if He wore comfortable shoes.

You own different kinds of aprons and you know what functions to wear them for in the church basement kitchen: a serving apron, an anniversary apron, the wedding apron, your everyday apron and, in an emergency, the dishtowel apron.

You have a box filled with organdy aprons given to you for your labors as a waitress at a classmate or cousin's wedding.

You realize that white dishtowels are very practical and can be used as headgear for kids playing Joseph in the Sunday School Program, a tourniquet for Mrs. Thorvald Olson's mishaps, a strainer for egg coffee grounds, and as sturdy rags for dusting off the old <u>Black Hymnals</u> that have been collecting dust in the store room since 1958.

You secretly know that some Lutheran Church Basement Women have been known to wash the church dishtowels with a load of dirty diapers.

You wonder if a cakewalk doesn't border on gambling.

You wonder if the Lutheran Church basement kitchen in heaven will have a gas or electric stove, and who will be in charge of the blown fuses and pilot lights.

YOU KNOW YOU ARE A COUNTRY CHURCH LUTHERAN IF . . .

YOU KNOW YOU ARE A COUNTRY CHURCH LUTHERAN IF ...

You know who the first pastor of your church was and his middle initial, who the founding fathers were and how they were related, and which family donated the land for the church, cemetery and parsonage.

Someone still rings the bell before Services start and on New Year's Eve.

No one has a key for the church because there isn't one.

Your organ is still pumped manually.

You kind of think of the organist's husband as one of the Minor Prophets.

Your organist is older than Methuselah.

You are pretty territorial about which pew is yours.

The janitor brings a Thermos of warm water from home for baptisms.

You have never questioned why there are sometimes only eight women in the Triple Trio.

You have at least two aunts who sing in the Triple Trio.

The hymn, **Work for the Night is Coming**, really speaks to you.

No matter if you are inside the church or out, you "smell barn".

You are certain that there won't be any mustard, burdock or pigweed growing in the fields in heaven.

You had an aunt for a Sunday School teacher and two cousins in your class.

You don't even notice that you had to wade through two inches of dead Junebugs to enter the church.

You go duck-hunting before Services on Sundays in the fall.

You believe that going deer hunting takes precedence over attending Church Services.

You agree that Services will have to be delayed so everyone can help chase the adjoining property owner's cows back home.

You don't know what Quinquagesima and Septuagesima mean, and you don't much care because you feel there are more important things in life.

There are kids of many ages in one Sunday School or Confirmation class.

You didn't question the relevance of memorizing commandments about coveting oxen.

You attended a high school that had a Junior-Senior Banquet in the church basement instead of a Junior-Senior

Prom at the school gym.

Your April bulletin has special announcements about lost four-bucklers and misplaced stormcoats.

Your husband's most recent suit is called his funeral suit.

You have wondered if the natives seen

on filmstrips have ever heard of fly-swatters.

You sometimes feel that the missionaries should censor some of the filmstrips shown at Family Night.

You are curious, after reading about Noah's Ark being constructed from gopher wood, who got the bounty for the claws? Ham, Shem or Japheth, or did they split it equally?

You worry that the new blue silo on Arnie Jensen's place will be taller than Prairie Lutheran's steeple.

You consider John Deere Day almost a church event.

You know that farmers are closer to God than city folks are.

You really only expected the hired men in the township to clean up and show up for Easter, Christmas and the *Lutefisk* Supper and you didn't pressure them to tithe.

You think the Mission Committee's

global Heifer Project could be moved a little closer to home.

There is an announcement in the bulletin requesting that members dump their used oil on the gravel road that runs past the church.

You think about the slough and ditches near Sven Tingblad's north forty when the gospel reading is about Moses in the reeds and bullrushes.

You vote to purchase Oscar Peterson's old Butler Bin for a maintenance shed at the cemetery.

You've been a member of the Cemetery Board for just about 40 years.

You know, without a doubt, that the Cemetery Board is more powerful than the Church Council.

You can tell the ethnic origin of the deceased by the spelling on the end of last names on the tombstones, ie., son, sen, ssen, sson, ston, etc.

You know who the founding father show-offs were by the size of their cemetery monuments.

You know that good works won't get you into heaven, but perfect attendance might.

You think that if the church is the Congregation of Saints, God must have a vivid imagination.

You bring leftover twine to church to be used for tying the storm cellar door shut or to be used around a bathrobe as a shepherd's fashion accessory.

You're pretty sure there is a Bible verse in some obscure Old Testament book that says, "Thou Must Have a New Easter

Dress and a New Christmas Dress Every Year".

There is a Mason jar filled and labeled "Fly Poison" sitting on the linoleum kitchen counter.

You know that joining Ladies Aid is not an option.

You recognize that a Potluck isn't really pot luck because you know what everyone is going to bring, how many it will serve, and whose food not to eat.

You understand the dangers of sitting on a recently varnished pew in a Dacron dress on a hot, humid August day.

Your church grounds have a couple of

permanent port-a-potties.

A NOTE ABOUT
ETHNIC LUTHERANS . . .

A NOTE ABOUT
ETHNIC LUTHERANS...

*You firmly believe that German Lutheran kids
who are lucky enough to attend college
should go to either Valparaiso or Wartburg,*

Finnish Lutheran kids belong at Suomi College in Michigan, Swedish kids should attend Gustavus Adolphus College, Danish Lutheran kids should go to Dana, well-mannered Free Lutheran kids should — after a stint at either LBI or Medicine Lake, depending on the era — attend Augsburg College, and that the other Norwegian Lutheran students can choose among as many Norwegian Lutheran-founded colleges as there are dialects in Norway: St. Olaf, Luther, Augustana in Sioux Falls, Concordia in Moorhead, Pacific Lutheran for the grandchildren of the Midwesterners who left during W.W. II for the armaments factories near Seattle, and yes, Augsburg College even though it is located in the heart of the Upper Midwest's Sin City.

YOU KNOW YOU ARE A NORWEGIAN LUTHERAN IF ...

YOU KNOW YOU ARE A NORWEGIAN LUTHERAN IF...

You think it goes without questioning that the Norwegians were the chosen ones.

You secretly keep looking for the phrase, "8 Goths and 22 Norwegians" in the Old Testament.

You agree that the books of the Old Testament have a bang to them, but you aren't sure they should be called a "cannon".

You think the phrase, Norwegian

Lutheran, is a bit redundant.

You sometimes wonder if Martin Luther wasn't really born in Norway and moved to Germany, but then you realize that wouldn't make any sense at all so you just keep it in your heart and ponder upon it now and then.

You don't think a pastor is worth his salt

unless he can preach in the Mother Tongue and does so at least twice a year.

You can spell and pronounce properly church names such as *Trefoldighet, Evighet, Vang, Bruflat, Aal* and *Norunga* and you know what they mean.

You can pronounce first and last names that began with *Hj, Kj* and *Kn.*

You can both spell and pronounce John Ylvisaker's name and you had a cousin who went to a Lutheran college with one of his relatives.

You think the song title, **I Was There to Hear Your Borning Cry**, is too risqué to have a place in an Augsburg Fortress publication.

You secretly wonder who put Song of Solomon in the Bible.

You know what valley the ancestors of everyone in the congregation came from in the Old Country.

Your grandson starts talking about "valley girls" and you start dreaming about *Hallingdal, Numedal,*

Gudbransdal, Setesdal, etc.

You can't figure out how Hans Nielsen Hauge and Marty Haugen could come from the same ethic background.

You are leery of anyone named O'Leary who joins the congregation.

You've secretly wanted to suggest that

the congregation hire an Italian salesman to head up the Pledge Drive.

You are positive that if F. Melius Christiansen had been a Catholic the Pope would make him a saint.

You won't admit that **Children of the Heavenly Father** was written by a Swede and that **Away in the Manger** and **A**

Mighty Fortress were written by Germans.

You can sing all four verses in all four parts of **Beautiful Savior** without the hymnal even though the well-educated choir alumni from St. Olaf mess up the order of the verses.

Your favorite hymn is **Lord Dismiss Us**

With Thy Blessing.

You figure that Jesus said "*Vær så god*" and then prayed "*I Jesu Navn Går Vi Til Bords*" before the meal at the Sea of Galilee even though they didn't have a table.

You can rattle off "*I Jesu Navn*" just as fast as you can blurt out "Come Lord

Jesus".

You consider King Oscar Fishballs bona fide seafood.

You visualize manna as rounds of miniature *lefse* floating down.

You just assume that *lutefisk* and *lefse* are directly descended from the two fishes and five loaves at the Sea of Galilee.

You not only know where all the *Lutefisk* Suppers are held within a 75- mile radius but you know the dates, times and the wait period in the Sanctuary before the fish is served.

You know you are motoring in the fast lane when you have been to four *Lutefisk*

Suppers already this November and you still have two to go.

You won't take Swedish meatballs or rye bread at a Church Supper even though you know they are included in the price of your ticket.

After yet another merger debate you don't find it unusual at all that the inventor of dynamite (Alfred Nobel) was a Swede.

You believe that the only secular group that can meet in the church is the local Sons of Norway group.

You find it almost unbelievable that "contemplative" and "contemporary" come from the same root word.

You firmly believe that Swedes and suicides should be buried outside the cemetery fence.

The Bible verse, "Revenge is mine. I will repay," keeps playing over and over in your head and you wonder how long it's going to take for Him to settle up with people.

Your husband's suit has a front pocket, not a breast pocket.

You fear that your daughter who attends St. Olaf College might fall in love with a boy from Gustavus Adolphus College and wonder what the founding fathers were thinking when they located the two colleges so close together.

You kind of wonder if LB and AAL merged only because it seemed like a trendy thing to do for Lutheran institutions.

You even wonder if AAL and LB matched funds for the building of Solomon's Temple.

You know which *stavekirke* your

grandfather was baptized in and hope to go there some day on a Sons of Norway Tour.

You really wonder, but never ask, where pastors' kids come from, or how in the world the pastor's wife got p.g.

You can sing all the verses of **Den Store Hvite Flok** in the mother tongue.

You have the motto, "Cleanliness is next to Godliness" *rosemaled* on your kitchen wall and you wish a few of your neighbors did.

YOU KNOW YOU ARE A SWEDISH
LUTHERAN IF . . .

YOU KNOW YOU ARE A SWEDISH LUTHERAN IF...

You think it goes without questioning that the Swedes were the chosen ones.

You feel that *torsk* is a good substitute

for *lutefisk*.

You can't understand why the Norwegians wouldn't make white sauce for their *lutefisk*.

You think mustard is a staple for every well-equipped church kitchen.

You visualize manna as little

pepparkakor coming down.

You continue to search for the word "coffee" in the Bible.

You feel that the next hymnal should be yellow and blue.

You feel a close kinship with King Gustavus Adolphus during a

Congregational Meeting because he, too, sang hymns during battle.

You know perfectly well who Caroline Sandell Berg was.

You just know that the favorite song of the Concert Choir in Heaven is **Children of the Heavenly Father.**

You would like to see "Top '40s" Casey Kasam pit **Children of the Heavenly Father** against the Norwegian's **In Heaven Above**.

You have never been to a funeral where either **How Great Thou Art** or The **Old Rugged Cross** wasn't sung.

You get a little annoyed when a

Norwegian wins a Nobel Prize.

You let your mind wander during Services and when you look at the cross in front of the church you dream of Maypoles and fair young maidens.

You tell everyone Mamie Eisenhower was a Swede, even though you didn't vote for her husband.

You brag about Jenny Lind, the Swedish nightingale, but you don't tell anyone that Greta Garbo and Ingrid Bergman were Swedes because of their Hollywood connections.

You faithfully ate Pea Soup and Pancakes on Thursdays until someone told you it was a tradition that went back to the time when Sweden was Catholic. So, after learning your history you switched to eating Chicken Noodle Soup and *Wasa* Crackers just to make a point.

You still put an almond in your rice pudding at Christmas even though your daughters have been married for over 30 years, and your granddaughters don't have any interest in getting married or in rice pudding.

You think everyone knows what *Ostkaka* and rennet tablets are.

You truly believe that Sankta Lucia wasn't an Italian, but a shipwrecked Swedish Viking woman who hitchhiked home to Sweden in time to help out with the Christmas cleaning and baking.

You still feel the need to get up at 4:00

a.m. when it is pitch-black out and 40 degrees below with winds whipping at 33 m.p.h. to milk 24 head of cattle so you have time to crank up the old car, load all six of you in it and head five miles down the road to be cheerful in a cold wooden church where you joyously sing **När Juldagsmorgon Glimmar** on Christmas morning.

YOU KNOW YOU ARE A DANISH
LUTHERAN IF . . .

YOU KNOW YOU ARE A DANISH LUTHERAN IF . . .

You think it goes without question that the Danes were the chosen ones.

You have a model boat hanging from the ceiling in the sanctuary that is usually full of dust.

Your favorite liturgical season is Pentecost because the altar cloth and banners are red and white.

You think *æbleskiver* can hold its own to *rømmegrøt* any day.

You have all the Bing and Grondahl royal blue Christmas plates way back to 1895 and all the Royal Copenhagen Christmas plates way back to 1908, and even though your kids buy them for you every year, they show no interest in your collection.

You have an irresistible urge to put a little mermaid on the edge of the baptismal font.

You allow your Sunday School class to play with Legos, but not Tinker toys.

You're not real happy that people interchange the words "snuff" and Copenhagen.

You know that not all Great Danes are dogs.

The intertwined rings on the altar cloth at a wedding make you think more about *kringla* than romance.

You realize that if Denmark had only kept Norway, Norway's oil money could have gone a long way to make up for unfulfilled pledges.

You always dreamed of having Victor

Borge give a free concert for Family Night.

You can accurately pronounce the name of Eksjø Lutheran Church.

You feel that a trip to Tyler and Aaskov, MN or Elk Horn, IA is akin to a pilgrimage to the Holy Land.

You couldn't be prouder of Søren Kirkegaard and have tried several times to trace your ancestry back to him.

You wish Kirkegaard would have spent as much time writing hymns as he did philosophy.

You think the Garden of Eden must have been located at Tivoli.

You get a little queasy trying to shout the Good News from the highest peak given the elevation of your Fatherland.

YOU KNOW YOU ARE A FINNISH LUTHERAN IF . . .

YOU KNOW YOU ARE A FINNISH LUTHERAN IF...

You think it goes without question that the Finns were the chosen ones.

You think St. Urho would have made a dandy Pope.

You think March 16th should be a national and religious holiday.

You actually eat chocolate-covered grasshoppers and pretend that you like them.

Your pastor asks that a *sauna* be installed at the parsonage and you don't bat an eyelash.

You don't think the church kitchen is too hot or steamy no matter how many pots of water are boiling.

You don't see the need for a humidity control button on the church thermostat.

You roll around naked in the snow and then into a hole in the ice after jumping out of a steaming *sauna* where you were flogged by a birch branch and think it's not only normal but about as close to the final rapture as one can get here on earth.

You wonder if, instead of baptizing a baby in the usual way, you couldn't just steam him up some.

You just assume that the tree Zacchaeus climbed and perched in was a birch tree.

You secretly do the tango with your husband in the living room when all the shades are pulled even though you know it's a sin.

You have a fond place in your heart for words like *"sisu,"* *"suomi"* and "apostolic."

You have no doubt that Sibelius is better than F. Melius.

You wiggled a little more than usual in high school history class when your teacher discussed socialism and were thankful it was never discussed in Confirmation.

You hate to admit that the various Norwegian Lutheran Colleges are responsible for the popularity of the hymn, **Lost in the Night**.

You proudly keep a copy of <u>The Kalevala</u> next to the family Bible in your living room even though you can't read it and don't really understand it when it is explained.

YOU KNOW YOU ARE A GERMAN LUTHERAN IF...

YOU KNOW YOU ARE A GERMAN LUTHERAN IF...

You know it goes without question that the Germans were the chosen ones.

You know for certain that if Martin Luther would have been elected Pope and lived in the Vatican, his wife Kitty would have invited the LWML over for a house tour and a light lunch.

You're pretty sure Walther would have been a Pope in his time too.

You think all Missouri Synod Lutherans are Germans or German wannabes.

You can be pretty well assured that anyone with the name Ole Olson won't be President of the Missouri Synod Church anytime soon.

You know that Dr. Martin Luther didn't directly evangelize to the Scandinavian Countries because it would certainly have come back to haunt him from the grave.

You figure the Scandinavian Lutherans must be mighty good freeway drivers because they are so experienced at merging.

You're pretty sure St. Louis is as sacred as the Vatican.

You know your "higher ups" are usually related from way back, but you're not sure if they were all called.

You believe your Concordia College is certainly different from the ELCA one in Moorhead, MN.

You understand what the "Office of the Keys" is.

You don't even flinch when passages

about submission are read from the pulpit.

You wonder if somewhere back in history your forefathers didn't get the words "baccalaureate" and "bacchanal" mixed up.

You think a sense of humor is one of the seven deadly sins.

You know you'd rather eat *kraut* than *lutefisk* any day.

You know your parochial school kids are not only more apt to be "lifers" in the church than those who went to public school, but also better basketball players.

**YOU KNOW YOU ARE
A CONTEMPORARY
LUTHERAN IF ...**

YOU KNOW YOU ARE A CONTEMPORARY LUTHERAN IF . . .

You don't think the phrases "Liturgical Dance" and "Lutheran Bishop" are oxymorons.

You can actually get excited about issues like the Concordat, Episcopalians, the Role of the Laity and decade-long studies on anything controversial.

You volunteer to design a web page for your congregation and actually see some merit to it.

You feel that the organ needs a couple

big amplifiers attached to it with a strobe light up above it and actually go to the Council to request funding for the project.

You think that Christian Country is a legitimate form of music.

You think that guitars and drums are as appropriate for Church Services as the

coin-operated pop machine in the
Fellowship Hall.

You see swaying and clapping in church
as legitimate forms of praise.

You don't get dizzy or feel off-kilter
when you enter a sanctuary that has more
than one aisle.

You don't think twice about phrases like Japanese Lutheran Church, Puerto Rican Lutheran Church, etc.

You can't imagine why someone hasn't formed a Marty Haugen Fan Club and you feel it just might be your calling and Christian duty to do so.

You think nothing of letting your kids

color during Worship Services and see some value in Children's Sermons.

You guiltlessly buy a frozen Dairy Queen cake with a computerized portrait of your son as frosting instead of spending two days whipping out a homemade, white, real Confirmation cake with seven-minute frosting that takes 45 minutes to make.

You think it's perfectly normal for your son to wear bulky Nike Boing shoes when he is an acolyte and also think it's okay for your daughter to not only acolyte, but to wear sandals without nylons, and eye shadow to boot, when doing it.

You have never had to feel guilty about skipping Luther League to attend 4-H or about skipping 4-H to attend Luther League.

You never blinked an eye when your kids wore shorts in the summer and jeans in the winter to church.

You say things like, "Won't you please share with us how you felt..." and are perfectly comfortable both saying this and sharing your own feelings.

You've never heard the words beseech, besmirch, backbite, stricken, smitten and afflicted.

You don't know the importance of words like "circles," "poured" and "turned."

You have no clue what the initials LBI or

CLBS stand for.

You think the quilting group should bring its finished products to an Art Fair.

You bring *salsa* for a condiment to the Fellowship Buffet instead of beet pickles to the Potluck Supper.

You have never heard of egg coffee and

decide to donate a *cappuccino* machine to church.

You get stared at when you call a hotdish a covered dish.

You think nothing of bringing a dish to the Fellowship Buffet that has *tofu* or curry powder in it.

You see nothing skimpy or trendy about bringing a vegetarian dish to church.

Your mind is open enough not to see the contradiction between being a practicing vegetarian and actively supporting the church's Heifer Project.

You never knew that church bulletins were really hotflash fans in disguise.

**YOU KNOW YOU
ARE RAISING A
CONTEMPORARY
LUTHERAN IF ...**

YOU KNOW YOU ARE RAISING A CONTEMPORARY LUTHERAN IF . . .

You buy your kid a Gameboy for a Confirmation gift instead of a Bulova watch.

You tell your son you had to memorize all of Luther's Small Catechism and repeat it back to the pastor in 15 minutes and he looks at you through his dyed blond bangs and asks, "Why?"

You feel in your heart that your son needs a traditional Confirmation haircut but he reminds you that from all the pictures he has seen Jesus had long hair and He turned out all right.

You comfort yourself with the fact that you don't have to tell your Confirmation-aged son about the birds and the bees, shaving, or what dancing can lead to as you watch him jump on his skateboard, grab hands with a long-haired, maroonish-colored blond wearing something that looks like a midriff only shorter on their way to who knows where. You just cross your fingers and your heart and pray . . . even if you are a contemporary Lutheran.

You tell your son about the horrors of Public Questioning or Catechization and he wrinkles his nose, shrugs his shoulders and facetiously asks, "What planet did you come from? Why didn't your Confirmation Class take a trip to Valley Fair or Seven Flags instead?"

You ask your son if he thought deeply about the meaning of life and the life hereafter at Bible Camp and he says, "Heck no. It was Bible Camp. We watched videos and had slam dances."

You then ask your son if they made

lanyards or popsicle stick crosses and
had greased watermelon contests at
Camp and he just walks away.

You ask him what Book of the Bible they
studied at Camp that week and he says,
"Either the Book of Abraham or the
Book of Adam. One of those old dudes."

You ask him if he got extra K.P. for not

having his bed made and he says, "I was at Bible Camp, not Boot Camp. The cleaning agency from town was there before I finished shaving and gelling my hair."

Your child has never carved a cross out of an Ivory Soap Bar.

Your kid doesn't blink when he sees a

dance listed on the agenda from the National Youth Conference.

You have never told your kids to "Stay away from the heathens" when they went to the County Fair.

Your teenager thinks Amos was a black rapper.

Your kid thinks breaking bread means getting change for a $50 bill.

Your son doesn't know that "original" sin means one that preceded all others; he thinks it means one that is new and unique and he spends most of his time trying to come up with some.

Your son compares Samson to Arnold

Schwarzenegger and says that Saul was so tall he could have been a center in the NBA.

After listening to a sermon about Madonna, the Virgin Mary, he says, "How dumb does Pastor Jamie think we are? Madonna sang **Like a Virgin** back in the '80s. I mean, the songs old, but it's not ancient history Bible stuff."

You tell your grandson about the book, *Kitty, My Rib* and he cheers, "You go, girl!"

ABOUT THE AUTHORS

Janet Letnes Martin and Suzann (Johnson) Nelson are two one-hundred percent Norwegian Lutheran Farm Girls who didn't turn and who didn't dance and who memorized all of Luther's Small Catechism, and it wasn't so small then. This is most Certainly True.

Janet and Suzann have co-authored 9 books, four of them dealing with their Lutheran heritage: <u>They Glorified Mary, We Glorified Rice</u>; <u>Luther's Small Dictionary, from AAL to Zululand</u>; <u>Growing Up Lutheran</u>; and <u>You know You Are A Lutheran If . . .</u> .

The other five books — <u>Cream Peas on Toast</u>; <u>They Had Stores, We Had Chores</u>; <u>Is It Too Windy Back There,</u>

Then?; _Uffda, But Those Clip-Ons Hurt, Then;_ and _Just How Much Scrap Lumber Does A Man Need To Save?_ — deal with their rural Norwegian-American heritage.

Their award-winning book, _Growing Up Lutheran,_ received the **Minnesota Book Award for Humo**r in 1998 and is presently being made into a musical.

Janet and Suzann often team up as a comedy duo, **Those Lutheran Ladies**, and perform their routine nationwide. In addition, these two hotflashing women speak individually or together for churches, conventions, festivals and many kinds of organizations. Their subject matter is growing up Norwegian Lutheran in rural areas, and their performances are always humorous – humorous, but true and touching.

Suzann runs a mail-order business called **Rural Route Bookstore** *which features Scandinavian-American, rural, regional and immigrant literature. She has edited several books including <u>Our Beloved Sweden</u> and <u>Helga Hanson's Hotflash Handbook</u> which were written and published by Janet.*

Janet and her daughter and son-in-law, Jenny and Steve Green, own the **Scandinavian Marketplace** *store in Hastings, MN as well as a mail-order business.*

Janet has co-authored three books with Allen Todnem of Hastings, MN; <u>Cream and Bread</u>, <u>Second Helpings of Cream and Bread</u> and <u>Lutheran Church Basement Women</u>.

She also co-authored the book <u>Our Beloved Sweden</u> with her sister, Ilene Lorenz, and wrote <u>Helga Hanson's Hotflash Handbook</u> and <u>Shirley Holmquist and Aunt Wilma, Whodunit</u>.

To book a program by **Those Lutheran Ladies** *call:*

    Jenny Green at: 651-437-4261   *or*

    email: Lutheranladies@aol.com   *or*

    write: Box 396, Hastings, MN 55033

MORE ABOUT "THOSE LUTHERAN LADIES"

Several of our books, especially *Growing Up Lutheran*, have been made into a successful musical comedy called *Church Basement Ladies.* To find out more about the play, or to order more of our products, visit our Web sites. We feature Scandinavian and Scandinavian-American products.

SCANDINAVIAN MARKETPLACE
www.scandinavianmarket.com
218 Second Street East
Hastings, MN 55033
651.438.9183 or 800.797.4319
Owned by Janet, her daughter and son-in-law

RURAL ROUTE BOOKSTORE
www.ruralroutebookstore.com
Suzann's online store is headquarted in Grand Rapids, MN 55744
Call 800.494.9124 or send inquires to questions@ruralroutebookstore.com

ORDER FORM *for* <u>YOU KNOW YOU'RE A LUTHERAN IF</u>...

*Name*_____

*Address*_____

*City*_____*St*_____*Zip*_____

*No. of Copies*_____ @ *$10.95*   *Subtotal* $_____

Plus Postage & handling (per book) $_____
$9.95 – $19.95 $4.95
$19.95 and over $5.95
MN Residents add 6.5% Sales Tax $_____

                                        Total: $_____

Send cash, check or money order to:
    Caragana Press, Box 396, Hastings, MN 55033

Order by telephone or email:

Contact Janet at:

 1-800-797-4319   *email her at: Lutheranladies @aol.com;*

or

Contact Suzann at:

 1-800-494-9124   *email her at: sbnelson@mchsi.com*

Both have different catalogs and Web sites.

To book a program by <u>Those Lutheran Ladies</u>:

Call Jenny Green at: 651-437-4261

 email her at: Lutheranladies@aol.com

 Write to her at: Box 396, Hastings, MN 55033

ORDER FORM *for* <u>YOU KNOW YOU'RE A LUTHERAN IF</u>...

*Name*_____

*Address*_____

*City*_____*St*_____*Zip*_____

*No. of Copies*_____ @ *$10.95*   *Subtotal* $_____

Plus Postage & handling (per book) $_____
$9.95 – $19.95 $4.95
$19.95 and over $5.95
MN Residents add 6.5% Sales Tax $_____

                                        Total: $_____

Send cash, check or money order to:
   Caragana Press, Box 396, Hastings, MN 55033

Order by telephone or email:

Contact Janet at:
   1-800-797-4319   *email her at: Lutheranladies @aol.com;*
or
Contact Suzann at:
   1-800-494-9124   *email her at: sbnelson@mchsi.com*

Both have different catalogs and Web sites.

To book a program by <u>Those Lutheran Ladies</u>:

Call Jenny Green at: 651-437-4261

   email her at: Lutheranladies@aol.com

   Write to her at: Box 396, Hastings, MN 55033